Nineteenth Century America

THE
RAILROADS

written and illustrated by
LEONARD EVERETT FISHER

Holiday House · New York

Library of Congress Cataloging in Publication Data

Fisher, Leonard Everett.
    The railroads.

    (Nineteenth century America)
    Includes index.
    SUMMARY: Traces the growth of the railroads
during the 19th century.
    1. Railroads—United States—History—Juvenile
literature. [1. Railroads—History] I. Title.
II. Series.
TF23.F57   385'.0973   79-1458
ISBN 0-8234-0352-1

List of Illustrations

TYPICAL LOCOMOTIVE WITH COWCATCHER

ON MONDAY morning, May 10, 1869, the United States of America, thirty-seven states at peace with each other, was still a divided country. Although no longer politically fractured North and South by civil war—the war had been over for four years—America was split, nevertheless. The division now was East and West— geographically, economically, developmentally.

The industrial, populous East, especially the Northeast, undamaged by war, still aglow with victory and reaching for progress and profit, was crisscrossed by a fast growing network of railroads. None of these railroads had been there forty years before. Most of them appeared in the 1850's and 1860's. These lines carried passengers and freight westward to the banks of the Missouri River—to Council Bluffs, Iowa—a distance of about 1200 miles from the Atlantic shoreline. Boston, New York, Philadelphia, Baltimore, and Washington, D.C. were linked by rail to the burgeoning midwest cities of Chicago, St. Louis, Kansas City, St. Joseph, and, of course, Council Bluffs. All of these lines fed into one another in a continuous web of iron and wood.

Among the Northeast lines of the day were those four major railways that in time would control all the others to the edge of the Mississippi River: the Baltimore & Ohio whose original thirteen miles of track laid in 1830 made it America's oldest continuing railroad, the New York Central, the Erie, and the Pennsylvania.

In the midwest and along the Great Lakes were all those lines that by 1895 would be incorporated into the systems controlled by the B & O, the New York Central, the Erie, and the Pennsylvania. Among these were the Michigan Central; the Michigan Southern; the Central Ohio; the Marietta & Cincinnati; the Pittsburgh, Fort Wayne & Chicago; the Ohio & Mississippi; and the Terre Haute & Indianapolis.

There were scattered rail lines in the South as well. These connected the coastal cities of Richmond, Wilmington, Charleston, and Savannah with such inland metropolises as Memphis, Atlanta, and Chattanooga.

One line, the Illinois Central, founded in the 1850's and destined for a legendary place in American history, ran north and south between Chicago and New Orleans. On the night of April 30, 1900—the twentieth century was just four months old—one of the Illinois Central's best engineers, John Luther "Casey" Jones, rammed his *Cannonball Express* at more than one hundred miles an hour into a stalled freight train near Canton, Mississippi.

> *Come all you rounders if you want hear*
> *The story told about a brave engineer.*

Casey died instantly in the twisted wreckage of his once magnificent "iron horse," Locomotive No. 382. The steam engine had been a powerhouse marvel on ten wheels. Although the crash cost him his life, Casey Jones' quick action and braking skill prevented a far worse accident and any additional loss of life. He could have jumped as he had ordered his fireman, Sim Webb, to do. Webb lived. But Casey hung on and earned himself an eternal niche in American folklore.

> *Casey Jones! Mounted to the cabin,*
> *And he took his farewell trip to that promised*
> *   land.*

In any event, at midcentury or thereabouts, a traveler could board a train in New York and reach Rock Island, Illinois, via Chicago, cross the Mississippi River into Davenport, Iowa, on the Rock Island Railroad Bridge owned by the Chicago & Rock Island Railroad Com-

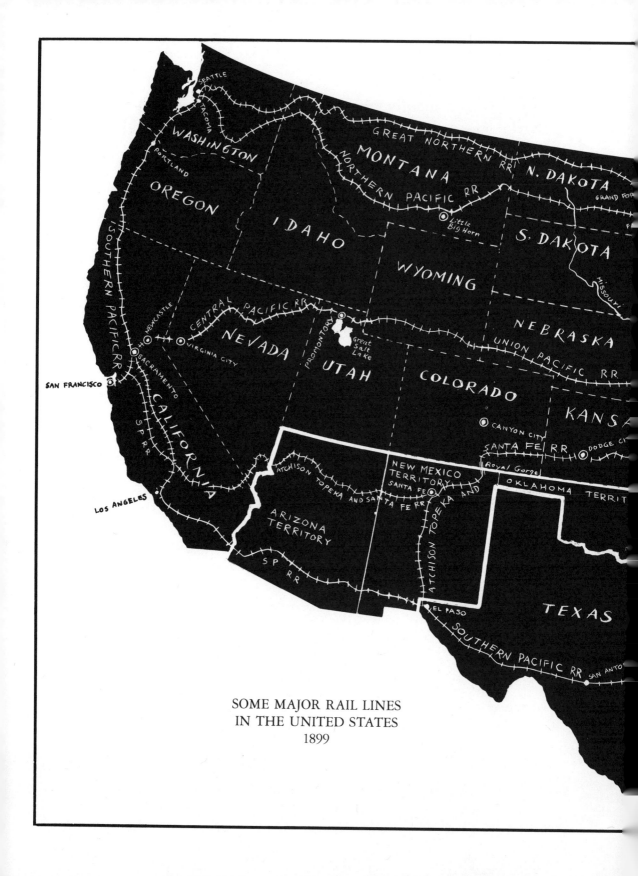

SOME MAJOR RAIL LINES
IN THE UNITED STATES
1899

pany, and arrive in Iowa City four or five days later.

It was one thing, however, for the owner-builders of the Chicago & Rock Island Line, Henry Farnum and Thomas C. Durant, to bring the iron horse to the river's edge. It was another thing to get the railroad across without floating it on barges. A bridge—a railroad bridge, the first to span the mighty Mississippi—had to be built.

Time and again riverboat men complained about the idea. They claimed it would be an obstruction to navigation. Urged by southern steamboat owners, southern politicians in Washington tried to prevent the bridge's construction. These steamboat owners saw their freighting business disappearing in the box cars from the East. Businessmen from one end of the Mississippi to the other whose commercial well being was tied to the north-south river traffic, viewed the east-west crossing of the railroad as a threat to their establishments. All of these interests, North and South, whose livelihoods depended on river transit rather than rail, sensed that the encroachment of the railroad further and further west would destroy the chances of any one of a number of great Mississippi River cities to become the commercial and cultural center of the nation. Moreover, southern agricultural hostility to northern industrial aggressiveness was about to foment an agonizing civil war. Southerners envisioned an inability to get their products to market if river traffic died. Worse still, they saw a South strangled by Northern railroads. Sooner or later there would be more east-west rail bridges across the Mississippi. And one day there would be railroads from California to New York creating large commercial and cultural centers at either end. Chicago already loomed as the pivotal clearing house for the nation's bounty with railroad tracks radiating in every direction.

None of the protests prevented the construction of the 1500 foot Rock Island Railroad Bridge. On April 22, 1856, the first passenger train to cross the Mississippi River rolled across the bridge into Davenport, Iowa. Two weeks later, a double-side-wheeling steamboat slammed into the bridge and blew up. The explosion destroyed part of the bridge as well.

STEAMBOAT HITTING ROCK ISLAND RAILROAD BRIDGE

The owners of the vessel sued the owners of the bridge, Farnum and Durant. They claimed that the bridge was a hazard to navigation. Farnum and Durant retained Abraham Lincoln, a reputable forty-eight-year-old lawyer. Lincoln argued that the boat was crippled before it hit the bridge; that it had drifted into the collision course with a structure that could not move out of the way; that the boat was to blame for the collision and not the bridge. Some railroad people hinted that the whole thing was staged so that the courts would have a reason to prevent the building of railroad bridges across any part of the Mississippi, but nothing ever came of that.

Lincoln made it very clear to the rest of the country that railroads had every right to travel east, west, north or south; that boats had the same right; that neither had the right, however, to interfere with the continuous transit of the other; that rails were to a train what water was to a boat; and that if a bridge was necessary to get a train over a river then that bridge had a perfect right to be there. Lincoln won his case.

The suit received nation-wide attention. The decision was upheld by the Supreme Court in Washington, D.C. When Abraham Lincoln was elected sixteenth President of the United States, two years later, in 1860, he entered Washington by train on the B & O. By that time the Chicago, Rock Island & Pacific Railroad—a new and more ambitious name—had begun to inch its way some

250 miles further west to Council Bluffs, Iowa—to the eastern bank of yet another river to cross, the Missouri. On the other side of the river was Omaha, Nebraska.

Council Bluffs was as far west as anyone could go by regularly scheduled passenger train on the morning of May 10, 1869. Council Bluffs was the end of the line— the very edge of mechanized civilization. Kansas City and St. Joseph, both end-of-the-line rail depots farther south in Missouri, were not as far west as Council Bluffs, falling short by only a few miles.

Travelers to the Pacific coast and places in between detrained at Council Bluffs, provided they took the Rock Island Line out of Chicago. There they crossed the Missouri River on flatboats, coming ashore at Omaha. They continued their way west by ox-drawn wagon, stage-coach, horseback, muleback, keelboat, river raft, or on foot. Whatever the mode of travel, the trek west beyond Omaha could take weeks or months should the traveler complete the journey in one piece—alive!—having survived storms, accidents, sickness, heat, cold, Indians, stampedes and starvation.

Between the Council Bluffs-Omaha area and the roaring surf of the Pacific Ocean lay the sparsely populated, undeveloped West. There stood soaring mountains with icy, snow-packed passes; endless plains and prairies; wind-whipped canyons, wild rivers, timeless meandering streams, and withering desert heat. There, too, roamed the countless herds of bison, cattle, and wild

Rock Island line was carefully made with all this in mind. Even before "Crazy" Judah had caught the transcontinental rail fever, Durant had persuaded the Omaha Indians to sell to him their ancestral lands on the western side of the Missouri opposite Council Bluffs. He called the ramshackle town "Omaha," after its former owners. From there he would lay 1500 miles of track to San Francisco. Omaha had become the perilous outpost of one man's ambition and one country's destiny—"the manifest destiny of the people to move westward," said Abraham Lincoln.

On July 1, 1862, President Lincoln signed into law the Railroad Act, resolving the issue of a transcontinental railroad and the route it would take. Lincoln and his generals were uneasy over the possibility that the Confederacy, with whom they were at war, could launch a strong attack upon the Union from California with help from western sympathizers. With a transcontinental railroad, troops could be moved west quickly to meet the challenge. The idea had been discussed for years. Everytime it came before the Congress, southern representatives and senators blocked it. They were not against a transcontinental railroad. They were opposed to such a railroad with a northern route. They wanted a southern route. With the outbreak of the Civil War, southern legislators left the Congress, thus leaving no obstacle to the creation of the railroad with a northern route.

Under the terms of the Railroad Act, two lines were awarded construction contracts: the Central Pacific, which had not yet laid a single track; and the Union Pacific, which until then had not existed. Subsequently, Thomas Durant managed to gain control of the newly organized Union Pacific before it too had laid a single track.

Work began in 1863 at both ends of the proposed line—at Sacramento and at Omaha. One year later and despite unimaginable difficulties (for example, equipment had to be brought by sea to California from New York by way of the southern tip of South America) the Central Pacific offered the public a thirty-mile service between Sacramento and Newcastle. The run took anywhere from an hour and fifteen minutes to an hour and forty-five minutes, with stops at Junction, Rocklin, and Pino. Omaha, Nebraska, was still 1500 miles and five days rail journey to the east, if the rails were there to travel on.

By the afternoon of May 10th, 1869, the rails were there! Omaha, Nebraska, was no longer eastern America's outpost in the West. By that afternoon, at a desolate spot on the northern rim of the Great Salt Lake in the Territory of Utah, some 850 miles due west of Omaha, and about 650 miles northeast of Sacramento—at a place called Promontory—America "East" joined America "West." The two halves were stitched together by the tracks of the Union Pacific laid westbound out of Omaha by an army of Irish immigrants, ex-slaves, and veterans; and the tracks of the Central Pacific laid eastbound out of Sacramento through the snowclad

Sierra mountains—sometimes at the rate of ten miles in a single day—by some five thousand Chinese laborers.

America now had a railroad that stretched from the Atlantic to the Pacific—a transcontinental railroad. And the ceremonies that took place that day at Promontory, in the Utah Territory, marked one of the biggest nationwide celebrations since the British surrendered at Yorktown, Virginia, in 1781, after the final battle of the Revolutionary War.

After missing their first strokes before a hooting crowd of laborers, drunks, shady ladies, professional gamblers, some dignitaries, a couple of brass bands, and soldiers of the 21st Infantry Regiment, Leland Stanford —now ex-governor of California—and Thomas Durant pounded gold and silver spikes into the last tie. The transcontinental railroad was a national fact of life. A wire attached to one of the spikes was meant to send the blow of the silver-headed sledgehammer across the country by telegraph. It did not work. A telegraph operator in Omaha picked up the Promontory message "done" and tapped out the "blows" to the rest of the nation himself.

"1869 May 10th 1869 . . . GREAT EVENT," proclaimed the vivid ornate poster. *"Rail Road from the Atlantic to the Pacific . . . GRAND OPENING of the UNION PACIFIC . . . avoiding the Dangers of the Sea . . . LUXURIOUS CARS & EATING HOUSES . . . PULLMAN'S PALACE SLEEPING CARS . . ."*

MAY 10, 1869, AT PROMONTORY

America exploded in a merrymaking din of bell-pealing, whistle-blowing, cannonading, singing, shrieking, parading, and prancing as the Central Pacific's locomotive No. 119 and the Union Pacific's *Jupiter* nudged each other. Great crowds in Chicago, Buffalo, Philadelphia, New York, Boston, Washington, D.C., San Francisco, and Sacramento took to the streets and congratulated each other. America, awash in a sea of pride and patriotism, whiskey and whoopee, celebrated her new unity while the happy throng at Promontory climbed all over the facing locomotives and had its picture taken. Photography was as new and as wonderful as the railroad.

Five days later, May 15th, the first transcontinental rail service was opened to the public. The trip took some 10 or 12 days depending on weather, breakdowns, and other troubles. Fares westbound from Omaha ran between $40 for a hard bench to $100 for a luxurious sleeper—George Pullman's "Palace Sleeping Car"—especially built for the new transcontinental railroad era. These fares doubled if the journey was full length, New York to California. They did not include meals taken in the undistinguished "eating houses" that lined the tracks westward or eastward. Plush dining cars, called "hotel cars," did not appear until the 1870's.

Trains made frequent stops crossing the country. They handled freight and mail, took on water, and allowed time for passenger "necessities." These frequent stops, together with an average speed of about 25 miles per hour, gave the passengers an unhurried look at the seemingly endless American landscape and the life that roamed its environment, chiefly cowboys and Indians, shaggy buffalo, lowing cattle, and howling coyotes.

It took six years to build the transcontinental railroad between Omaha, Nebraska, and Sacramento, California. None of it was easy. Road beds had to be carved out of the rugged Sierra Mountains at dizzy heights and angles. Tunnels had to be blasted through those mountains. Crude, wooden, tunnel-like "snowsheds" had to be built to protect tracks, trains and work crews from gigantic snowslides and drifts. Many a Central Pacific laborer lived in these windy, frigid snowsheds as the difficult work went on. Throughout this continuing struggle men died. They died of disease, by accident, from bullets and tomahawks.

A SNOWSHED

The white man, having made specific treaties with the great Indian nations of the West, marking off tribal lands and defining ownership, rewrote those very same treaties whenever convenient—or wherever the railroad went. Lands once solemnly deeded to the Indians by the United States government were invaded by the white man's "iron horse." The United States government did little to protect the interest of the Indians in this matter. The angry Indians attacked the railroad at every opportunity. There were too few federal troops in these areas to protect the railroad builders, and the Indians carried off many a scalp. They gave up their own lives in return. It did them little good, however. The railroad and civilization clanked on as the hostile Indians, unable to cope with their changing world, and unwilling to accept intruders upon land they considered their own from the beginning of time, were pushed onto smaller and smaller undesirable tracts or "reservations."

By the 1880's, there were four other transcontinental railroads chugging across the West in addition to the Central Pacific-Union Pacific lines: the Atchison, Topeka & Santa Fe; the Northern Pacific; the Great Northern; and the Southern Pacific. The building of all these lines met fierce challenges from the driven Indians—Sioux, Crow, Blackfeet, Arapaho, and Cheyenne, to name a few of the tribes. But it was the Sioux opposition to white settlement and the laying of Northern Pacific tracks in the Dakota and Montana Territories that provided one of the most celebrated annihilations in United States military history.

During the 1870's, President Ulysses Simpson Grant ordered the army to protect western settlers and railroad builders. Indian attacks on both had become more furious. The President had to insure completion of the railroads most of all. In calling out the army, the federal government was responding to a variety of pressures, including business interests impatient with territorial

A TRAIN UNDER ATTACK

settlement. They wanted no further delays in the expansion of the West. There were vast areas of rich, raw materials to be brought out of the West, and these raw materials, such as lumber, minerals, ore, and grain, were becoming more necessary to the economy of the nation which was moving swiftly toward full industrialization.

The fast-growing population in the East and Midwest, thickened by European immigrants, had to have a steady supply of meat, among other staple foods, for their tables. Meat was a body-building food for those who stoked the furnaces of the mills, refineries, and factories upon whose steady production the country had become more dependent. America was no longer just a farming community. Large segments of the population used the railroads to leave the farms to work in the mills, refineries, and factories of the cities. Meat had become an essential part of their diet. Railroads could bring western cattle to the Chicago stockyards and slaughterhouses more cheaply and quickly than any other means of transport. And from there, from Chicago, the butchered and dressed meat would find its way by rail again to the shops, stoves, and dining tables of the American working family.

Accordingly, President Grant reacted to the nation's mood to have complete control of all its contiguous territories from the Atlantic to the Pacific. He ordered General Alfred H. Terry to squeeze the troublesome Sioux and Cheyenne onto confining reservations. No further obstacles to the building of the Northern Pacific Railroad and the West would be tolerated. Included in the military expedition was the crack 650-man Seventh Cavalry Regiment, United States Army, under the command of a noted Indian fighter and Civil War hero, Lt. Colonel George Armstrong Custer. George Custer, sometimes known as "Long Hair" to the Indians, who despised him, was often referred to by his army rivals as "Boy General" or "Glory Seeker." He was not altogether popular among his own military comrades, either.

GEORGE ARMSTRONG CUSTER

On Sunday, June 25th, 1876, ten days before the United States would celebrate its 100th birthday, Custer, riding into the Montana Territory on General Terry's orders, sighted an Indian encampment, which had been reported previously by army scouts. Seemingly small, it was quietly nestled in the valley of the Little Big Horn River. Thinking that he was outnumbered only a little less than two to one—perhaps 1000 Indians as opposed to his 650 troopers—and seeking the advantage of surprise, Custer quickly divided his regiment into three columns. He sent the first column under Captain Frederick W. Benteen to the hills on his left to protect his flank. He sent Major Marcus A. Reno with the second column charging directly into the camp. He himself led the third column of some 225 men into the hills on his right, aimed at attacking the encampment from the side.

But there, in those hills to his right, Custer met his doom with stunning finality. Five thousand Indians, meeting in a great war council called by Sioux Chief Sitting Bull, rose up out of the Little Big Horn and wiped out the column to the last man. The fight "did not last long enough to light a pipe," according to Indian veterans of the massacre.

For the Sioux Chief, Sitting Bull, and his lieutenants, Chief Crazy Horse and others, the battle, known as "Custer's Last Stand," was the most momentous victory ever won against the white man. But the Battle of the Little Big Horn, the results of which were not known for some ten days, proved to be without strategic merit in the Indian war against the onrush of industrial civilization. The white man went on pursuing the Indians with more vigor, overwhelming them with the iron horse.

Over the stretch of railroad-building years in western

CHIEF SITTING BULL

America, however, it was not the army or the Indian fighters that ultimately weakened the Indians' will to resist, rendering them incapable of winning. It was hunger that sapped their fighting spirit and allowed the railroad to creep across the plains.

In the late 1860's, a Kansas meat contractor, supplying a dwindling food ration to the railroad workers, hired a crack-shot ex-pony express rider to shoot some buffalo and replenish the meat supply. His name was William F. Cody, soon to be known forever as "Buffalo

A BUFFALO HUNTER

Bill." Cody was so good and so fast a hunter that he could drop a dozen buffalo with almost as many shots—on the gallop—before a fairly competent hunter could take aim. Nearly single-handedly, Buffalo Bill fed the army of rail workers with his smoking rifle. It became fashionable to hunt buffalo—even from the windows of moving trains—and few people sensed the possibility that the buffalo could disappear from the American continent. Worse still, few cared that the starvation of the Indians over the cold winters was directly linked to the killing of the buffalo to feed the hungry railroad builders.

"A good Injun is a dead Injun," could be heard in every rail town that rose on what once was Indian land.

In the twenty year period between 1865 and 1885, an estimated twelve million buffalo were slaughtered. What the hunters did not kill, what the Indians themselves did not kill, the people on the onrushing trains destroyed.

The fighting and the killing along the railroad tracks was not confined to white men versus red men and buffalos, however. The railroad workers fought among themselves. Pitched battles were not uncommon in the seedy little wood and canvas towns that sprung up at the edge of the newly laid tracks. Hard and dangerous work by day spilled into the crowded, rowdy saloons at night. There, a river of whiskey, too few dancing girls, restless cowboys too long on the range, and any number

nearly $150,000 in their packs, the gang was caught. They were locked up on a train and sent to Seymour, Indiana, to stand trial. They never arrived. A band of angry horsemen stopped the train, yanked off the gang, and hanged them all from trees that lined the tracks.

Not long after the Reno gang was summarily executed by a public that took the law into its own hands, that very same public had a change of heart. Outraged by the high prices railroad companies were charging for the sale of public land that had been given to them at little or no charge by the federal government, the people began to think of train robbers as avenging heroes.

The most famous of all these desperado-heroes were the James brothers, Frank and Jesse. Between 1873, when they held up the Chicago, Rock Island & Pacific at Adair, Iowa—about thirty-five miles east of Omaha, Nebraska—and left a dead engineer, and 1881, when a price was put on Jesse's head, the gang terrorized western railroads at will. The James "boys," which included such other surly characters as Cole and Bob Younger, and Robert Ford, robbed a few banks as well, until the Younger brothers were shot and captured. Frank, Jesse, Ford, and a few new hands, however, had better luck with the unprotected, lonely railroads.

The railroads hired private detectives—"Pinkertons" —to find, arrest, and break up the James gang. But they were resisted by a public who, because it viewed itself

TRAIN ROBBERS

more victimized by greedy railroads than by train robbers, refused to cooperate. Frank and Jesse James became more difficult to find and apprehend, because those who actually knew of their whereabouts—including some lawmen—remained silent. Railroads were the villains, not hard-riding bandits whose derring-do was being regularly romanticized in dime novels everywhere.

Finally, in April, 1882, while living under the assumed name of "Howard" in St. Joseph, Missouri—everyone there knew who the "Howards" were—the James gang came to the end of its thieving career. Jesse was shot in the back of the head by his erstwhile partner in crime, Robert Ford. Ford betrayed Jesse to collect the $5000 reward put on his head by the governor of Missouri.

> Jesse leaves a widow to mourn all her life,
> The children he left will pray
> For the thief and the coward
> Who shot Mr. Howard
> And laid Jesse James in his grave.

From that day in May, 1869, when the transcontinental railroad became an American fact of life at Promontory, Territory of Utah, few rail lines escaped brutalization by train robbers. This was especially true in the West and Far West where long stretches of un-

JESSE JAMES

FRANK JAMES

guarded, isolated track invited attack.

In no time at all railroad officials, sensitive to the gold, silver, and payroll shipments aboard their trains, became more alarmed over the thieving bent of American bandits than they were over the murderous attacks by marauding Indians. The Indians were not as interested in the money as they were in preventing the white man and his railroad from suffocating them. They would destroy the white man and his railroad wherever they could. The white train robber, on the other hand, was interested only in snatching money and not in wrecking the railroad, although a wreck or two in the interest of a well-planned robbery was never ruled out.

Much of this was quickly driven home to the rail operators on the occasion of the first robbery on the transcontinental line.

On November 5, 1870, an eastbound Central Pacific train out of Sacramento, California, carrying passengers and a $40,000 payroll for the miners of Virginia City, Nevada, was stopped on the California-Nevada border in the dead of night. There, some robbers removed the entire payroll. On the night of November 6, 1870, the same train was stopped again. This time it was on the Nevada-Utah border, some 350 miles from where it had been halted only 24 hours before. Again it was robbed of still another sum of money, by a different gang.

Travel back and forth on the western leg of the transcontinental railway was nothing less than a struggle of life and death. Those who dared to take the trip challenged the elements; the efficiency of the engine that hauled them to wherever it was they were going; the sullen, terrifying Indians; the villainous drifters who plagued the various stops; the wild railroad workers "out on the town" with a week's pay in their pockets, giving passengers good cause to lock themselves up in their cars and draw the shades; and, last but not least, those masked desperados who derailed and shot up trains to rob them and their passengers of as much of their worldy goods as could be carried off. Hardly a train left a depot without an armed guard in the baggage car and armed passengers sitting nervously in their seats.

But whatever it was that compelled Americans to travel the country by train—business, adventure, a new life, new experiences, sightseeing, or those hair-raising exploits they read about in those countless dime novels —they boarded the trains by the thousands, bags and baggage, and moved by rail in every direction, north, east, south, and mostly west.

OLIVER EVANS' AMPHIBIOUS DREDGE

FROM THE very beginning of steam power in America, nearly the entire young country was caught up in a fever for steam mechanics. Oliver Evans invented the first steam-powered dredge in 1804 for use on Philadelphia's Schuykill River. But only a few visionaries considered the possibilities of hauling goods and people everywhere around the nation with a steam engine on wheels having "a velocity of 100 miles an hour," according to John Stevens. To prove his point, Stevens built a locomotive and ran it on a circular track in Hoboken, New Jersey, in 1825.

At about the same time that Evans had his steam engine working, an English mine owner, Richard Trevithick, built the first workable railway steam locomotive to haul coal out of his mine. In 1825, another Englishman, George Stephenson, built and drove a steam loco-

40

motive that successfully pulled some 30 cars loaded with coal, flour, and people at seven or eight miles an hour along a stretch of track in Northern Ireland owned by the Stockton & Darlington Railway Company. The age of the common railway carrier—the era of transporting passengers and freight by rail over long distances—was about to begin in Europe. America was not far behind.

Between 1800 and 1825, the principal arteries of travel in America were unreliable dirt roads and natural waterways. Eastern businessmen were frustrated by the high cost and considerable length of time it took for shipments of western raw materials to reach the Atlantic coastal communities. Western trade flowed more easily into the Mississippi River than in their direction. An abundant network of rivers was connected to the Mississippi, but the Appalachian mountain range stood as a solid impasse to free-flowing trade routes. The goods and products that were shipped overland through those mountains went by horse and wagon.

In order to increase the trade flow between the Mississippi River and the Atlantic Ocean, reduce the high cost of shipping, and thus lower prices for a growing consumer demand, artificial waterways—barge canals—were dug in Pennsylvania, New York, and elsewhere.

In 1825, what had been a three-week wagon trip from Buffalo, New York, to Albany, became a one-week barge trip on the newly completed Erie Canal. The 360-mile canal connected Lake Erie with the Hudson River—the

Great Lakes with the Atlantic Ocean—the western United States with the eastern United States. The shipment of raw materials from the West through the Great Lakes to Buffalo, through the Erie Canal to Albany, and then south via the Hudson River to New York City was faster and less costly than ever before. The route made the East the manufacturing center of the country. It made New York City a commercial center and eventually the financial capital of the entire nation.

Four years after the opening of the Erie Canal, on August 8, 1829, in a quiet corner of northeastern Pennsylvania, Horatio Allen, a Delaware & Hudson Canal Company engineer, drove a steam locomotive, the *Stourbridge Lion,* along a sixteen mile track from Honesdale to Carbondale. The Delaware operated coal mines in Carbondale. It constructed its own railway to haul coal to Honesdale in horsedrawn wagons. There, by means of a company-owned canal system, the coal was shipped to the Hudson River.

Allen had been sent to England to study the successful use of steam locomotives on coal mine railways. The Delaware & Hudson Canal Company was anxious to have him improve its transport methods. Allen was so convinced that the British steam locomotive was in his company's future that he brought four back to America, including the *Lion.*

Over the next few years railroads began to appear in

various parts of the East, North and South. But while enthusiasm ran high for them, resistance began to grow. America was undergoing a change in her outlook. About 50 years after being a colonial possession of Great Britain, the United States was beginning to change from an agricultural society to an industrial nation. The railroad was not only something of a symbol of that change but an instrument for change as well. The railroads would create a different life for those near

STOURBRIDGE LION

the new lines. And some places, once thriving but soon to be out of reach of the railroads, would be facing harder times.

A few Charleston, South Carolina, businessmen, realizing the possible importance of a railway that could transport their large cotton crop to market, formed the South Carolina Canal & Railway Company in 1827. In 1830, they built a track between Charleston and Hamburg, and ran a train between the two cities. The train was powered either by a sailcar or by a horse working a

BEST FRIEND OF CHARLESTON

treadmill, but neither technique proved to be efficient. Then they hired Horatio Allen to find a better way. He did and had a New York foundry build a steam locomotive.

The locomotive, the first ever built in America, and called *Best Friend of Charleston,* went into service December 25, 1830. For six months it hauled passengers and freight back and forth between Charleston and Hamburg at speeds of about 20 miles per hour. In June, 1831, it blew up killing the crewman who mistakenly shut down a pressure valve. For a number of years following the disaster railroad promoters had a difficult time convincing a frightened public that railroads using steam locomotives were good for them and here to stay.

Local laws were passed to prevent railroad companies from building their lines through towns that did not want them. Usually, these laws were instigated by inn-keepers or tavern owners and other small businessmen who depended on stagecoach owners and drivers, and canal users for their economic well being. They would always call attention to the South Carolina tragedy and the loss of life. On occasion, civil engineers surveying land tracts for railroad routes were run off that land by sharpshooting people who objected to the coming of the railroad. In some areas where short lines managed to operate, tracks were torn up and engine crews shot by snipers. Once in a while a train was permitted to run on Sunday if it scheduled church services on board.

On August 25, 1830, a few months before the *Best Friend of Charleston* was put into service, the Baltimore & Ohio Railroad tested a small steam locomotive designed by a New Yorker named Peter Cooper. The engine was so small—one horsepower and one ton—that it was named *Tom Thumb,* after the miniature storybook character. The B & O had been founded by Baltimore merchants in 1827, the same year the South Carolina Canal & Railway Company was chartered. Like the Charleston businessmen, the Baltimore group had business problems. The two-year-old Erie Canal in New York had effectively cut into their trade with Ohio. Baltimore business interests decided to lay their tracks straight into Ohio and draw off trade then heading toward Lake Erie and New York.

Until the trial run of *Tom Thumb,* the 13 miles of B & O track were devoted to horsedrawn cars. But on its trial run, the tiny locomotive proved that it could easily

TOM THUMB

pull a passenger car with less wear and tear than a horse. Horses on that line had to be changed at a halfway point some seven miles down the track. *Tom Thumb* needed no rest or changeover. On its return trip, however, having made the first test of thirteen miles successfully, the small engine with its attached passenger car was challenged at the halfway point by a horse-drawn car on the opposite track. Racing toward the finish, the locomotive pulled ahead of the horse. Unfortunately, a mechanical failure caused the engine to lose power and the race. But the engineers on board the locomotive had seen enough. They and company officials were convinced that, with certain refinements, the "iron horse" would soon replace the real horse on railways and other public conveyances.

Apparently, there were others who held the same opinion. The fear of railroads and their engines began to wane. Rail lines sprouted all over the East. By 1835 there were at least a thousand miles of track throughout the East. Boston itself had three separate lines beginning to reach out toward the rest of the country.

The once pastoral landscape of America, quiet and undisturbed, was now pierced by the sight and sound of a mechanical marvel, the locomotive and its coupled cars. For some it was magical excitement that promised fairytale adventure. To others it was a shattering of an old and good social order, and the creation of a new and uncertain world.

Not too many years later, commenting on the transcontinental railroad, Emerson continued his romance with the railroad, echoing the sentiment of people everywhere: "And the Iron Horse, the earth-shaker, the fire-breather . . . shall build an empire and an epic."

Charles Dickens, the English author of *Oliver Twist* and other novels, was not altogether pleased with American railroading. In *American Notes*, written in 1842 while he toured eastern America by rail, Dickens complained: "There is a great deal of jolting, a great deal of noise, a great deal of wall, not much window, a locomotive engine, a shriek and a bell . . . The cars are like shabby omnibuses . . . insufferably close." He also noted that there were no first- and second-class "carriages" as in England. Instead, there were cars for men only—smoking cars—and for women only—non smoking cars. There were also cars for "negroes . . . as a black man never travels with a white one."

By the time the Civil War started in 1861—a war fought between a progressive industrial North and a conservative agricultural South—there were at least 200 operating railroads in America. The largest group of these ran in, around, and out of the Northeast. The second largest congestion of rail lines was in the Midwest in a great ellipse formed by Chicago, St. Louis, Cincinnati and Cleveland. There were a few lines in the South, and there was nothing but stagecoach service and pony mail express in the West.

As the Civil War raged on and bloodied the country, the railroads became a necessity of war life—and open targets. The North, with its vast network of track, used the rail lines to ship troops and supplies to the battle areas. The Baltimore & Ohio, being the closest rail line to some of the major Virginia battlegrounds, was subjected to constant harrassment by Confederate raiders and sympathizers. B & O tracks were demolished along with bridges, trestles, and other equipment. But the B & O would not give in. The company built an armored rail car and mounted a cannon up front to fight off unsuspecting raiders.

Flat cars were used to haul heavy mortars into firing positions. Other cars towed high flying observation balloons, used mostly by Federal troops to spot Confederate positions. Both sides, North and South, did everything possible to destroy each others' ability to move men and materiel. Thus the railroad with its depots, junctions, and miles of track became a prime target. Two of the South's most important rail centers, Richmond, Virginia, and Atlanta, Georgia, were devastated by Union troops, who made sure that not a single locomotive could pull a single car in or out of the smoking ruins.

By the war's end, Union forces were repairing damaged rail lines almost as fast as Southern troops could tear them up. The entire repair operation was under the direct field command of Brigadier General Herman

A UNION ARMY MORTAR

Haupt, former constructon engineer and general superintendent of the Pennsylvania Railroad. Another railroader, Brigadier General Daniel C. McCallum, former general superintendent of the Erie Railroad, was in charge of all military rail transportation for the Union.

The South, ill-equipped mechanically, poorly organized industrially, and lacking the technical expertise seeded in the manufacturing climate of the North, could not repair their damaged railroads in time to be effective. The Union army's military use and maintenance of the railroad rewrote the textbooks on modern warfare. The North's twenty thousand miles of track and its know-how in building, running, and maintaining operable or serviceable rail lines was a contributing factor to the South's defeat.

After the war, during the period 1865-1870, financially powerful railroad interests in Baltimore, Philadelphia, and New York resumed expanding their enterprises, an activity that began in the 1850's. Now the aim of these interests was to invest in other rail lines beyond their immediate grasp with an eye toward ownership, and to compete with one another for control of each other's railroads.

Among those who managed to consolidate and extend the eastern railroad establishment to Chicago and St. Louis, despite the hazards of stock manipulations, financial frauds, conniving, and court battles, were John W. Garrett of the Baltimore & Ohio; Erastus Corning

53

and Cornelius Vanderbilt of the New York Central; Daniel Drew, Jay Gould, and Jim Fisk of the Erie; and Tom Scott and Edgar Thomson of the Pennsylvania.

By 1880, all four lines controlled the rail routes between Chicago and New York, and Philadelphia and Baltimore. By 1895, both the Pennsylvania and the B & O had extended their reach as far west as St. Louis, Missouri.

But were it not for the mechanical ingenuity of the industrial nineteenth century American, no amount of financial wizardry and manipulation could have produced that wonder of wonders, the Iron Horse, the fire-breathing, earth-shaking, monster builder of an "empire and an epic" that took America where she wanted to go most of all—West!

Beginning in 1832 with a locomotive called *Old Ironsides*, Matthias Baldwin and his mechanics built more locomotives than anyone else. During his own lifetime, Baldwin, a Philadelphian, put 1500 steam locomotives on American rails. The company he founded went on after his death in 1866 to produce more than 60,000 locomotives. But more important than Baldwin's energy and engineering skill were the constant improvements he and others made on the locomotives that contributed to the quick and stunning growth of the railroad industry in America.

Robert L. Stevens, president of the Camden & Amboy Railroad that ran between Philadelphia and New

York City, designed an "H" shaped rail, called a "T Rail," in 1831. The T Rail was the model for all modern railroad tracks. In the early years of railroading, the tracks were simply straps of iron laid over lengths of wood. Stevens' innovation, however, was a rail of solid iron. These replaced the old strap iron track. By 1900, nearly every mile of the 200,000 miles of iron T Rails in America was replaced by steel T Rails.

Isaac Dripps, one of Robert L. Stevens' mechanics, introduced the bell and oil-burning headlamp on the locomotive. He was also responsible for the "cow-catcher," the protruding angular iron grate at the head

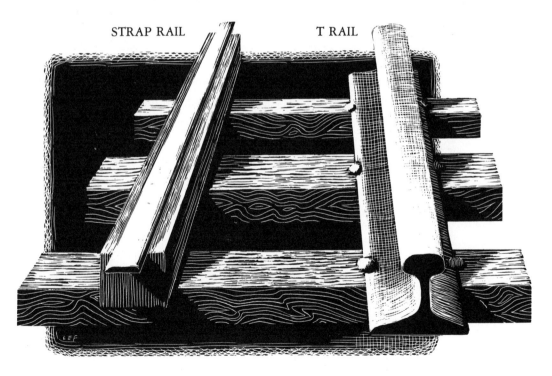

STRAP RAIL   T RAIL

of the engine used to nudge animals off the track.

Numerous smoke stacks were designed with or without flared shapes to reduce the shower of sparks that fell on the locomotive and the cars behind. These were also designed to prevent the sparks from igniting the countryside through which the train passed. Coal-burning locomotives used stacks called "Diamonds," "Shotguns," "Capstacks," and "Congdons." Wood-burning locomotives also used Diamonds in addition to "Sunflowers" and "Balloons."

By the 1840's, a weatherproof cab enclosed the engineer and fireman. The cab, mounted on the engine, permitted the crew to operate the locomotive in comfort, out of the weather.

By the 1850's, the telegraph, invented in 1844 by an artist named Samuel Finley Breese Morse, was in use directing the movement of trains. Also, whale oil for headlamps was replaced by kerosene, a brighter burning fluid that made night travel safer. By 1881, locomotives would have electric light headlamps.

In 1869, George Westinghouse invented air brakes for locomotives. The air brake allowed more sudden stopping, thus reducing the risk of collisions. Westinghouse went on to invent safety signals and other railroad devices. He was also responsible for introducing alternating current to America, a system of electric current delivery invented by Nikola Tesla. Alternating current was a less expensive system than Thomas Alva

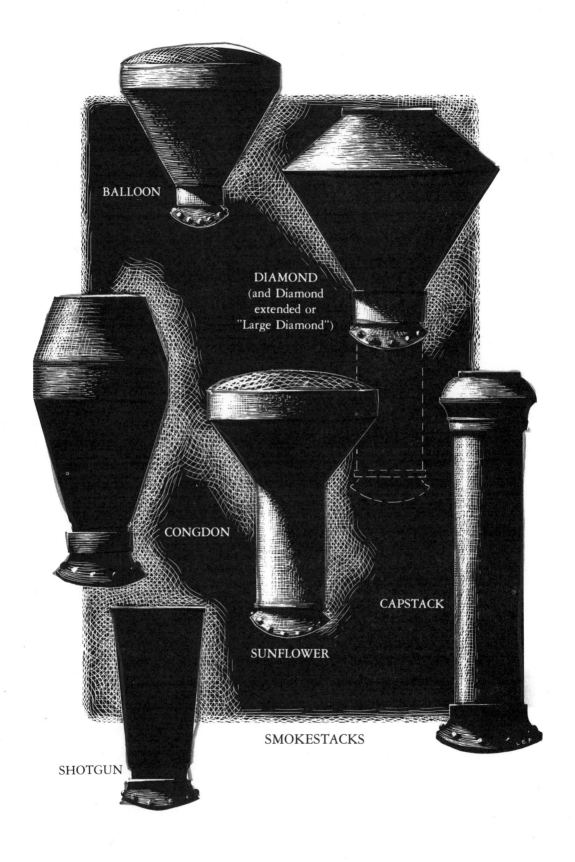

BALLOON

DIAMOND
(and Diamond
extended or
"Large Diamond")

CONGDON

SUNFLOWER

CAPSTACK

SHOTGUN

SMOKESTACKS

Edison's direct current and helped make it possible to bring cheap electricity into many American households.

In any case, these inventions and others so refined the operation of American railroads that railroading, considered to be a dangerous business earlier in the century, was no longer thought to be particularly hazardous by the end of the century.

If there were hazards, they were caused more by greedy management and investors than by mechanics or engineers. Toward the end of the 19th century, the business of railroads put great wealth in the hands of a few people. Such personal wealth and its continuing accumulation caused much unrest and discontent among the railroad workers—conductors, firemen, engineers, brakemen, signalmen, yardmen, and the like.

In 1877, the federal government had to call out some 10,000 troops to stop striking railroad workers, who were protesting pay cuts, from destroying the B & O and Pennsylvania Railroads. Dozens of people, soldiers and workers alike, died in the riots.

In 1894, similar violence broke out against the Pullman Company in Chicago. Pullman had declared a sizable dividend for its stockholders while cutting the pay of its workers. Then 100,000 people rioted and again troops were mobilized, and again people died. Most of these strikes and protests were failures in that the railroad employees did not get much satisfaction from their employers. Nevertheless, strong railway unions developed under the leadership of Eugene V. Debs, an official of the Brotherhood of Locomotive Firemen. These unions turned away from violence and sought the help of the government. The government, beginning with the administration of President Grover Cleveland, wanted no further violent demonstrations that disrupted the country's well being and cost lives. The Cleveland Administration wrote a series of investigative reports that set the foundation for future labor laws requiring a third party, a mediation board, to settle unsettled arguments between the railroads and the railworkers, between employers and employees.

Despite the turmoil present in a nation that had changed so fast and grown away from what it thought it still was—the wonderful timeless order of the Pilgrim Fathers and George Washington—America and her railroads pressed on. America was a new and different place that stretched from the Atlantic to the Pacific, from the Gulf of Mexico to the Great Lakes, and all tied together by railroads. America was a new spirit riding to glory on a railroad, flexing muscles she was not yet quite sure how to use. The symbol of that power and destiny that swept the people along in its excitement was the railroad and its steam locomotive.

The big engines lived up to John Stevens' early prophecy of traveling at speeds of 100 miles per hour. Although Stevens did not live to see the truth of his prediction, one of his contemporaries did live long enough. Horatio Allen, the engineer who piloted the *Stourbridge Lion* in 1829 at 10 miles an hour, lived to see the transcontinental streak across the plains in 1890 at nearly 100 miles an hour.

Many, like New England's Henry David Thoreau, who had originally resisted the coming of the railroad and the mechanization of society, finally came to terms with the inevitable rush of civilization.

Expressing his dislike for railroads chiefly because the Fitchburg Railroad—later to become the Boston & Maine—skirted too close to the edge of his Walden Pond, Thoreau wrote in 1854, "We do not ride the railroad; it rides upon us. Did you ever think what those sleepers are that underlie the railroad? Each one is a man, an Irishman, or a Yankee man. The rails are laid on them."

Later he would say, "When I hear the iron horse make the hills echo with his snort like thunder . . . it seems as if the earth had got a race now worthy to inhabit it."

And all America agreed.

Index